FRIVOLOUS VERSE

and worse

JOHANNES KERKHOVEN

TSL Publications

First published in Great Britain in 2022
By TSL Publications, Rickmansworth

Copyright © 2022 Johannes Kerkhoven

ISBN / 978-1-914245-84-8

The right of Johannes Kerkhoven to be identified as the author of this work has been asserted by the author in accordance with the UK Copyright, Designs and Patents Act 1988.

All characters and events in this publication, other than those clearly in the public domain, are fictitious and any resemblance to actual persons, living or dead, is purely coincidental.

All rights reserved. No part of this publication may be reproduced, stored in a retrieval system or transmitted, in any form or by any means without the prior written permission of the publisher, nor be otherwise circulated in any form of binding or cover other than that in which it is published and without a similar condition being imposed on the subsequent buyer.

Cover Design: Johannes Kerkhoven

*For Jean Hall, Rosanna Taylor and Judy Langton.
The four of us formed 'Poetic License'. We performed many
times at Upstairs at The Gatehouse, Highgate, London.
Also for the poet Dennis Evans, whose weekly teaching group
taught us lots.*

CONTENTS

Laughter 8
Magnetism 9
In Praise of Plumpness 10
Discretion 11
Acrostically Yours 12
Prayer on Awakening + Heredity 13
My Other Self 14
My heart Leaps 15
A Woman Like a German Clock 16
Point of View 17
Are You Loathsome Tonight 18
Adam and Eve + Promise 19
Your Lips + When the Wind Lies 20
Fast Ride to Heaven 21
Don't 22
Healthy Living 23
Temptation Please 24
Meeting or My Quest for Love 25
Wedding Night 26
Let Us Play 27
More Further Prayers 28
Fashion 29
Jack and Jill 30
Selfridges 31
The Card 32
Amsterdam Window 33
Early Morning Moment + Goosey, Goosey, Gander 34
Another Day Done 35

Cars 36
London Buses 37
Would You Believe It? + The Jolly Miller 38
Bakers Do Bake 39
Bird 40
My Best Friend 41
Blubbering Heights + Night Road 42
Wedded Bliss 43
The Proposal 44
The Old Master 45
Choirboys 46
Blue 47
Winter Interlude 48
Wasted Woolf Whistles 49
Crumbs 50
Daddy-Long Legs 51
The Spec Builder +
The Demise of the House of Lords 52
The Burly Cop 53
The Blue-arsed Blowfly 54
Naked and Cold 55
Obsession + Sing a Song of Millions 56
Published! 57
Teatime 58
ABC of Life 59
Getting Paid 60
Dysfunction 61
PC Poetry 62
The 32 Historic Churches of Norwich 63
Danger Zone 64
The Fly 65
Footwear Village 66
King Arthur 67

Call Yourself an Editor? 68
Politicians 69
The Diamond 70
A True Story 71
Getting Older 72
Christopher Tye + An Old Lady 73
Mary 74
Finger Play + Feeling Too Well 75
Poet's Lament 76
Do I Have To? + Dream Poetry 77
Little Bo-Peep 78
Unusual Pronounciations + Mrs 79
The ABC of War 80-81
The ABC of Love 82

SHORTS SECTION 83
Clerihews 84
More Clerihews + Edna Meena + Jack Horner 85
A Selection of Limericks 86-88
Jack Sprat + We Apologise + Rub-a Dub 89
It's Difficult + More Limericks + The Crab 90-92
Origin + Alone He Walked + A Masochist + The Eel 93
ABC – Names of Persons Limericks 94-101
ABC – Place Names Limericks 102 -114
Afterword 115
About the Author 116

MAGNETISM

I want to be a little magnet
stuck to your fridge door
then every day you'll look at me
just like you did before.

When things are taken from the fridge,
please, gently close the door
for if you slam it I'll fly off
and finish on the floor.

I might be trampled underfoot,
be face-down in the dirt
Or, with some luck, I'll fall face up,
So please don't wear a skirt.

In Praise of Plumpness

For me no
skinny
little frump
with bones
like dagger points.
Give me a lady
who is plump
with smoothly
covered joints.
I can't resist
a dimpled knee,
and firm pink
cheeks and lips.
A silky-soft skin
that's for me,
all over
ample hips.
Ah!
Rubens' ladies;
what delight,
big-breasted,
bare and bold.
Keep Lowry's
matchsticks
out of sight,
there's nothing
there to hold.
Thin feels
like half
of her's
not there.
Plump's always
gorgeous,
clothed or bare.

DISCRETION *(With thanks to Roger McGough)*

Discretion is no part of Valerie
and all of her is ice.
Her lips are sharp as razorblades,
her legs a human vice.
The very worst of everything,
she turns men into mice.
She'll whip and slash and torture you
with every known device.

She takes delight in hurting you,
it gives her life its spice.
And Valerie gives to her best friends,
the clap, the pox and lice.
She always without warning
will quote, then up her price.
Be careful when she feels you,
she might cut off a slice.

When in your blackest nightmare
you buy her merchandise
and feel like being wicked,
boy, then you'll pay the price!
And if you've lost your heart to her
(could happen in a trice),
you're lost, you're gone, you're hist'ry,
you're human sacrifice.

Valerie is contemptible
never known to be discreet
and only rampant masochists
would rate her as a treat.

ACROSTICALLY YOURS

Lead me into temptation
End my blasted expectation
And each day I'll sing your praise, Lord
Don't think it's a childish phase, Lord.

Make me meet someone just to sin
End this dreadful state I'm in.

I don't mind if she's thin or fat
Nor that her chest be big or flat
That I leave to you, who knows me.
Oh! To choose is hard. It throws me.

Therefore, hear my urgent prayer
Erotic nights no matter where
Make a lady want me badly
Praying works, I'm hoping madly
Then please get busy, do your best
Anyone who's passed your test
Temptation's what I pray for
I say there's nothing that I want more
Out of words now, I hope you care
Now's the time to hear my prayer.

PRAYER ON AWAKENING

Thank you, O Lord,
For creating me.
You could have made me anything,
But you made me English.
Perfect.

Thank you also for my rich parents
And for my beautiful body.
I marvel at my perfection in everything.
Is that why you made me a woman?

HEREDITY
with apologies to Thomas Hardy

I am the family face
I do not perish but will live.
And as I leap from place to place,
whatever life does give,
I always leave a trace.

In flesh and voice and eye
I've mocked the human span
and the endurance that is I,
is the eternal man,
whose face will never die.

MY OTHER SELF *with apologies to R L Stevenson*

I have a little Ego that goes everywhere with me
and what can be the use of it, well nobody can see.
I love it very much of course and it lives inside my head.
It's like another person and talks to me in bed.

The nicest thing about it is the way it likes to grow–
not at all like certain people, who can be very slow,
for sometimes it expands itself like an India-rubber ball,
it never gets much smaller, that wouldn't do at all.

It does not have a notion of how others like to play
and sometimes makes a fool of me, in a friendly sort of way.
It's always close to me, which gives me quite a charge.
Though sometimes I do wonder if it's not become too large.

One morning very early I woke and saw the rain.
I turned and yawned and closed my sleepy eyes again.
'You're much too good to go to work,' my lazy Ego said.
'You're right,' I yawned again. 'Today I'll stay in bed.'

MY HEART LEAPS

Oh, lovely Gail, you make me swoon,
You are my favourite tycoon.
My heart leaps up with all its might,
Out of my throat and out of sight.

On golden thread my fleeing heart
Is captured, caught by Cupid's dart.
(I sing at night to Gail; when I can dream
without low pangs of self-esteem.)

I am the frog that you bewitch,
It matters not that you are rich.
I can't control this love of mine,
If you have faults, that's also fine.

I'll fend for you, I'll mend for you,
I'm going round the bend for you.
My nightingale, my Holy Grail,
I love you quite beyond the pale.

I'll cook for you, I'll clean for you,
Please tell me what I mean to you.
My wings are clipped, my soul has flipped,
Of reason and of sense I'm stripped.

Such love should conquer everything.
So please be mine and buy yourself a ring.

In Love's Labour's Lost *King Ferdinand and his three courtiers swear to shun women for three years so they may study ancient Greek or Renaissance Italian philosophy. Biron denies being interested in any woman.*

"What? I love, I sue, I seek a wife?
A woman, that is like a German clock,
Still a-repairing, ever out of frame
and never going aright."

From Biron's* speech in Love's Labour's Lost,
*Norton p.760, 4.i.175-78.
I felt it was an unusual comparison – so I wrote this poem.*

A WOMAN LIKE A GERMAN CLOCK!?

Tick-a-tock, tick-a-tock,
a lady like a German clock.
Who is the lady in this song
and does she go cuckoo or go ding-a-dong?

Would she not live and love with great precision
and look at us with some derision?
For we, mere mortals, cannot match her chime,
and often cannot even be on time.

If she were mine, on Sundays she'd get wound,
for otherwise she would not sound.
and I, her husband, I would have the key.
Would she then tick-a-tock all day, and then all night
   for me?

I could be horological as well,
so that when she ding-dongs for me, I'd ring my bell.

POINT OF VIEW

One man sees poetry, another doggerel
One man sees scribbling, others a novel.

One man's aftershave is another's stink
One man's disaster is another's social drink.

One woman's hero is another's wimp
One woman's go-between is another's pimp.

One person's sacrilege is another's devotion
One person's pond is another's ocean.

One person's prince is another's frog
One man's master is another's underdog.
I could go on forever, what would be the point?
There's always someone with their nose out of joint.

Self-loathing. Might this, on occasion, be a creative force?
Asked Fergal Keane in Something Understood *(BBC).*
It seems a comforting concept.
I want to be loathsome and subject to a creative force.

ARE YOU LOATHSOME TONIGHT?

Aah now – the dear old BBC
has given me much hope.
They, in my self-made misery,
did teach me how to cope.

They've shown that my self-loathsomeness,
is a creative force.
I've reached my inner wholesomeness
and touched my inner source.

I have no friends, I have no kin
I hate my mum and dad.
I deal out insults with a grin
and misery makes me glad.

When meeting someone new, I'm rude
and show distaste and hate.
Jump, with my loathsome attitude,
straight in – why hesitate?!

So instead of getting tight,
Try being loathsome tonight!

ADAM AND EVE

I do believe in Adam and Eve
That was a great beginning
No work, all play, making love all day
There was no such thing as sinning.

They were great in their natural state
Warmed by a golden sun.
So what is the deal, what is the appeal?
Are apples really so much fun?

Luckily the snake did persist
Or none of us might exist.

PROMISE

You promised me we'd never part
When Cupid fired his lethal dart.
I felt as big as Bonaparte.
My happiness went off the chart
I thought and was – just like Descartes,
You were Ambrosia – à la carte.
But then you overturned the applecart
As casually you broke my heart
And I found out that you are a tart.

YOUR LIPS

Your lips, your hips, your tongue
it isn't right that they belong
to one who can and will
use love to maim and kill.

In every torrid dream
you taste of honey and of cream
I feel your arms, your hair
and then I wake on fire and in despair.

To fill the empty space inside my day
work is no help; I fritter life away.
If only I could send myself to sleep
forever and to dream and keep
the dream alive, to share your breath,
for with this pain my life is death.

WHEN THE WIND LIES

When the wind lies in the east,
She will call you a beast;
When the wind lies in the north,
You should not go forth;
When the wind lies in the south,
Kiss her cherry mouth;
When the wind lies west,
You may think of the rest.

FAST RIDE TO HEAVEN

My grandma rode a bright red bike,
Her stockings at half-mast;
Not caring to be lady-like,
That terror of Belfast.

At road rules she would spit and sneer,
Did wheelies lightning fast.
Mad yapping dogs would howl and fear,
That terror of Belfast.

She'd yell, 'Come on, cut out the talk!
I'll race you!' —And zoomed past.
She'd scatter all poor folk that walk,
That terror of Belfast.

Then grandma had her accident
We all were quite aghast.
She ran into a city gent,
That terror of Belfast.

She knocked that city gent for seven.
And grandma, yelling, went to heaven.

DON'T

Please don't be rude, your attitude
feels never quite correct.
You over-eat, and sometimes cheat,
don't always show respect.

You slump and slouch; can be a grouch,
you'll have that final drink.
You act the fool, show ridicule
and sometimes, well, you stink.

Hold in those farts, don't flirt with tarts,
throw out your cigarettes.
You burp and sneeze and sniff and wheeze,
and gamble and lay bets.

Please dress with care and comb your hair,
don't be a dirty slob.
So shine your shoes and flush your loos
but don't become a snob.

Yet still my sweet each time we meet
I'm utterly consumed by love –
So please delete all the above.

HEALTHY LIVING

You must take several vitamins
and cut off all the fat
from every bit of meat you eat.
We all should eat like that.

Yes, Aspirin is good for men
so take one every day
for just one tiny little pill
keeps heart attacks away.

Stand every morning on your head
for that improves the brain
and eating onions it is said
sends illness down the drain.

But chocolate weakens bones
so let that pass you by.
Although it's also good for you
I can't remember why.

How many coffees do you drink?
if you have more than three
your breasts may very well shrink.
But that won't bother me.

So let's promote a healthy life
Follow all the experts give.
But by the time you've done all that,
you won't have time to live.

TEMPTATION PLEASE

I'm cool with young mothers, don't curse them like others,
when I have to jump clear of a pram.
I don't spit in the street and prefer not to cheat
and would certainly never say 'damn'.

If I do break a cup, I will always own up,
and then offer to clean up the mess.
If you spilled some red wine on white trousers of mine
I would smile and demand no redress.

We know cats are quite thick, but when mine needs a kick
I relent and will give it a stroke.
I've stopped biting my nails and now only drink ales.
I'll help anyone who's broke.

So dear Lord, you can tell that I've done rather well.
My behaviour's been better than best.
So dear Lord if you're there and dear Lord if you care,
may I proffer a tiny request?

It's not money I need, I don't know the word greed
but I don't like feeling frustrated.
If you could fit me in, would you please make me sin?
I'd be much obligated.

MEETING
or
MY QUEST FOR LOVE

I met a beautiful Communist
and for two years I was dangerous
until she left me for a Capitalist.

I cried for a month but, being courageous,
I took up with a beautiful Buddhist
and sat in the lotus position for two years.

You don't see a lot sitting like that,
so when Heather clad in leather said, 'I insist,'
I'm on the back of her Harley and I saw me a lot.

One morning after coffee she rode off into the sunset.
Heather was desperately missed.
I felt incredibly lonely after that.

Then – a political lady whom I'd never met before.
wanted to be kissed. Instantly I knew. She's the one!
Now, what a life, all I do is canvas door to door.

WEDDING NIGHT

Downstairs and upstairs
To my lady's room.
It is our wedding day
And I am the groom.

But the room is empty
My lady is not there.
Upstairs downstairs
I searched everywhere.

Finally in the kitchen,
There my lady was
Sitting by the open fire
Trembling like a horse.

I said, 'I am wondering
Why are you still awake?'
She said, 'To do some pondering
And finish off the cake.'

'I had better help you,'
That is what I said.
When all the crumbs had gone
And many things were said
And another flask of bubbly done,
We tumbled into bed.

With apologies to Dylan Thomas
Prayer by the Reverend Eli Jenkins
from Under Milk Wood

LET US PLAY

Every morning when we wake,
Dear Lord, we frolic by the lake,
O please to keep Thy lovely eye
On awful folks that wish to spy.

And every evening at sun-down
We frolic 'neath our eiderdown,
For whether we are tired or no,
For that, we'll always find a mo.

We are not wholly bad or good
 But we're forever in the mood,
And Thou, I know, wilt be the first
To see our best side, not our worst.

O let us play another day!
To frolic each and every way,
Is what we aim for, slow and fast.
Yes, let us frolic till our last!

MORE FURTHER PRAYERS*

Every morning when I wake,
Dear Lord, a little drink I take,
O please to keep Thy lovely eye
on my half-empty flask of rye.

And every evening at sundown
I ride my pushbike into town,
and whether I last the night or no
depends on whether cash runs low.

No one is wholly bad or good,
I like a drop, that's understood,
but Thou, I know, wilt be the first
To understand my growing thirst.

O let us drink another day!
Bless us tonight, both straight and gay,
At closing time we'll all kow-tow
and say goodnight–but just for now!

Inspired by Under Milk Wood *by Dylan Thomas.*

FASHION

To wear a tie or wear a vest;
a suit or jeans like all the rest?
I like my parting on the right
as those of other gender might.

I will not wear a pony tail
nor see myself as total male
or shave off all my hair,
for dressing-up or down I will not care.

Armani, Calvin Klein or Fcuk
are names with which I hold no truck.
Fashions are, I read – unkind? –
for folks who can't make up their mind.

Though fashions do not mean a jot,
my clothes must be without a spot.
Imagine if by some unlucky chance
I travel in an ambulance.

To fashion, I prefer hygiene –
I am quite godly when I'm clean.

JACK AND JILL

Jack and Jill went up the hill
To fetch a pail of water.
Jack fell down and broke his crown
While Jill quite choked with laughter.

Jack got up and home did trot,
As fast as he could run.
But Jill decided, 'I will not,
I'm off to have some fun.'

That night to Annabelle's she went
And ordered beer and junket.
She met a politician, quite the gent
Who promised love and trinkets

Jill flashed a thigh but said, 'Dear sir,
I'm not that kind of lady.'
Then he bought her diamonds and fur,
Whereupon she said, 'Well, maybe.'

After a brief and passionate affair
He no longer wished to support her.
Broke, angry then and in despair
Jill phoned a Daily News reporter.

SELFRIDGES *(Apologies to John Betjeman)*

In the food hall at Selfridges
my love and I did meet
between the counters and the fridges
it's where she called me 'sweet'.

Her cupid lips were shaped for fun
A burnished gold her hair
her cheeks like peaches in the sun
all ready to ensnare.

Big shoulder pads and black she wore
all smart designer gear.
I saw her eyes and wanted more,
I felt my heaven near.

Her stockinged legs were metres long
and sleek for all to see.
I felt like bursting into song,
'Please, do come home with me.'

Next thing she's busy buying loads of food,
still smiling, nudged me gently,
'I hope you're in a giving mood.
I've left my money in the Bentley.'

I paid, kissed her goodbye and did my sums.
Great! Just enough for fish and chips at mum's.

THE CARD

I love you more than all the stars
and golden sun and moon
you're beautiful and kind and warm
but why must you sing out of tune

I love the way you walk and talk
I love the way you look
I love the way you dress and laugh
but not the way you cook

I love the way you smile at me
I love the way you touch
I love the way you hurry home
but not when you've drunk too much

I love the generosity
which sometimes you display.
And you told me that you love me
because it's Valentine's day

You're full of good intentions
without trying too hard.
But why each year do you have to mention –
That one year I forgot the bloody card!

AMSTERDAM WINDOW

You sat in a window on a bleak Saturday night
in a house in the district that's known as red light
what surprised me, my darling, you looked so content;
I asked myself wildly, did you know what this meant?

The light in the room was soft and diffused
and I was devastatingly, utterly confused.
Was it you? But of course, I walked forward and back
you still wore the ribbon that I tied around your neck.

Your eyes looked right through me, I was quite amazed
And called out to the windows that were double-glazed.
You got up and stretched and you then looked away.
That hurt and enraged me more than I could say.

I sprang into action with my thumb on the bell.
It rang loud and clear; I could hear it quite well.
Footsteps came closer and stopped at the door.
A huge hairy man growled, 'Yes?' He looked sore.

He took a step forward and I stuttered, 'That,'
I pointed, 'That's Angela, my runaway cat!'

EARLY MORNING MOMENT

The moon was in my sleepy eyes
Alight and twice its normal size
I wondered if my languid stare
Lay on its silver surface where,
You, noting its fair face by chance,
looked up and met my anxious glance.

The miles between us are untold,
but knowing that our hearts grew cold,
the tears we've shed in unison,
were what I'd never reckoned on.

I shook myself, then, on the point of crying,
I smelled the egg and bacon frying.

GOOSEY, GOOSEY, GANDER

Goosey, goosey, gander, whither shall I wander?
Upstairs downstairs in my lady's chamber.
There I met an old man who would not say his prayers
I took him by the left leg and threw him down the stairs

Then I tried to say my prayer
but my lady showed a pretty pair.
So I could not concentrate
felt my sins accumulate.

Now whenever I kneel beside my bed,
I can't get that chamber out of my head.
Hence each night before I'm sleeping
her sweet pair in mind I'm keeping.

ANOTHER DAY DONE

I wake at five before the light,
swing out my left leg then the right.
I totter round and boil an egg
and curse the stiffness in my leg.

As milk is spilled I burn the toast
glance at the mirror, see a ghost;
I'm sure I know him, but I swear,
he looks a lot the worse for wear.

I watch my hand shake; break a cup;
sleep through a movie then wake up.
It's time to eat and when I'm fed
and had my sweet it's off to bed.

CARS

I thought I was an amiable chap
but drivers often throw me in a flap.
Nonchalantly, loud-speakers blaring
they make crossing roads a feat of daring.

While one hand somehow manages to steer
the other holds the phone clamped to his ear.
Rounding the corner at hair-raising pace;
some feel they're at Le Mans and in the race!

I'm full of fear that they will run me down
so I will seldom venture into town;
always choosing a pedestrian street
and end up buying what I do not need.

When I get power over all the cars,
I'll banish every single car to Mars.
Up there their nasty horns can bleep-bleep-bleep!
They won't disturb a single person's sleep.
Battery flat and finally quite still,
they'll gently rust into a Martian hill.

Through telescopes the sharp-eyed may well spot,
cars like red rocks, each one a tiny dot.
They'll find the colour of the planet Mars
is quite identical to rusting cars.

LONDON BUSES

Driving a bus used to be a bore
not any more
those new buses are great
you can accelerate
and, unexpectedly, brake hard.

There's always one passenger
who doesn't hang on
instead of sitting down.

Best of all is the domino effect
one falls into the next and then the next . . .

At the depot we compare
it is quite rare
if a driver can't score
at least one passenger on the floor.

The record is ten
six on the floor downstairs,
and four on top.

WOULD YOU BELIEVE IT?

Office desks have 400 times more bacteria than toilet seats, according to a survey in New Scientist.
The Sun *21 Dec 2005*

So busy folk, all office workers
Don't have that sandwich at your desk
It might look clean, but we know better
So no tomatoes, salad, feta.

Don't turn your desk into a cafeteria
For lurking there are trillions of bacteria
So play it safe, I know I do
As from today I'm lunching in the loo.
And at my desk? Your guess, I'll leave it up to you.

THE JOLLY MILLER

There was a jolly miller once
Who lived on the river Dee
He worked and sang from morn till night
No lark did sound more blithe than he.

But t'was sad, the burden of his song
Forever used to be
'I care for nobody, no! not I,
As nobody cares for me.'

'You're wrong my dear,' said sturdy Sally Lee,
'I care for you, you silly old Moo.
If you would mill my grain for me
There's two warm round loaves for you.'

BAKERS DO BAKE

Bakers do bake but surgeons don't surge
Cobblers do cobble but sturgeons don't sturge
fishermen fish and teachers do teach
but a cardinal doesn't play cards on the beach.

Catchers do catch and bowlers do bowl
but do cricketers crick, does a Pole ever pole?
sellers do sell but do usurers use?
but refuse collectors, they do collect refuse!

Does a caterer cate or what midwife will mid?
We know a tiler does tile and bidder does bid,
Farmers do farm and we know cardsharps are sharp
but if carpenters carp will a harpist then harp?

These tricks of the language get invaders confused,
and at the same time it keeps us know-alls amused.

BIRD

I saw a little lady
    Come step, step, step,
I cried, 'Sweet little lady,
    I'm your chap, chap, chap.'

I went to the door and said,
    'Stay, stay, stay.'
But she shook her little tail
    and walked away, way, way.

So I got my little coat on
    and went step, step, step.
Then when I tried to kiss her,
    She went, slap, slap, slap.

I knew when I was beaten
    and was sad, sad, sad.
Then I went out to a party
    and was bad, bad, bad.

MY BEST FRIEND

All boys are lonely as a rule
at horrid ghastly boarding school.
But I was lucky at Scarlake
I found my one-eyed trouser snake.

I'm never lonely with my pet
And truer friend I've not yet met
He sometimes wakes me up at five
I stretch myself and come alive.

I'd stroke him gently and he'd grow
And warms me and it's then I know
That he will be my friend forever
We'll never part, not us, not ever.

BLUBBERING HEIGHTS

With us you learn to cry methodically
Your body will be balanced chemically.
Our workshops will connect you to your soul
Balanced biochemistry will make you whole.

Experience the happiness tears can bring.
Take your place in life and stop dithering.
So all who are sad or in a negative mood
Come to Blubbering Heights, the cry will do you good.

And if the crying therapy does not suffice,
Our laughter therapy is now half price.

NIGHT ROAD

I am a prince turned toad
Who walks along this slippery road
At three a.m.

When many blistering words were said
She threw me out of the marital bed.
'Tis very cold I am.

I found a meadow lush with clover
But then the farmer ran me over
And told me 'Scram!'

I'll sleep behind the Snail and Trout
On this vent where nice warm air comes out
Phew. Carpe diem.

Churches are more relaxed about the sanctity of marriage It's fine now to be divorced and same sex marriages are no longer news. In the US a man made an attempt to marry his horse. Where will it end?

WEDDED BLISS

My friend is wedded to a calf
He calls her his bovinely better half
In church he strongly said, 'I do,'
while, shyly, she replied, 'I moo.'

His parents were not pleased a lot
to live in sin though he would not,
for bride and groom it's always best
when their relationship is blessed.

They paid their money to the priest
and asked him to the wedding feast.
'Be blessed,' he said, 'but now agree
to bring your offspring up RC.'

THE PROPOSAL

Down Haverstock I walked along
with quietly measured pace.
I felt so happy, sang a song,
as autumn breeze caressed my face.

Yes life was good this crispy day
and Belsize Park was near.
I thought of how we planned to play
and what I'd whisper in her ear.

I hoped she wears her little dress
the one that's red and clings.
Yet vaguely anxious as I did progress;
does she have plans to clip my wings?

She said, a sparkle in her eye,
'Ah, would you like some tea?'
'I would,' I said, 'my throat is dry.'
'I'll warm the pot,' said she.
Then suddenly on bended knee
the dreaded question she did pop.
A terrifying thought came over me:
Oh dear, this time I'm for the chop.

Struck dumb I knew not what to say.
'Do think,' she smiled, 'while I make tea.'
The door was open and I sprang away.
This shave was one too close for me.

At whistling kettles I still jump with fear
Then, calming down, I shed a happy tear.

THE OLD MASTER

We've heard his poems all before
but always ask him for one more,
we wouldn't dream to interject
his voice, his diction, all perfect.

A lifetime of experience
does hypnotise his audience.
His words do penetrate our heart
we hold our breath for him to start.

He always enters with a glance
that puts his list'ners in a trance.
The pre-performance cackling stops
we almost hear the pin that no one drops.

He speaks of lovers lost, is asking 'Why?'
I feel a teardrop flowing from my eye.
I'm savouring the experience
but am disquieted by the audience.

There's whispering and a short soft cough.
I feel like calling, 'Stop, enough!'
Some start to chuckle and I wonder why
but then I spot the master's open fly.

CHOIRBOYS

Shining eyes in bright young faces,
angel sounds through teeth with braces,
voices sweet as demerara
sing Allegri's Miserere.

Master Jake, his voice quite brilliant,
sings his solo, pure and vibrant.
Then he stops, starts twitching, wriggling,
while the other boys are giggling.

Miss Primrose coos, 'Jake, are you ill?
I must insist, do please stand still!'

'I'm sorry, Miss,' says master Jake,
Still wriggling like a nervous snake,
'Some horror standing at the back
put itching powder down my neck.'

BLUE

A little blue man
with little blue feet,
stood nodding his brainpan,
right here in my street.

This little blue person
then opened my gate.
He said, 'I'm MacPherson,
I'm sorry I'm late.'

Then little blue person
split into four.
Each piece said, 'MacPherson,'
and rose from the floor.

These four little fellows
rolled into a ball,
yelled: 'We shall be yellows!'
and bounced out through the wall.

WINTER INTERLUDE

Fingertips tingle
Indigo sky stretches above
Nobody intrudes
God himself is nowhere to be seen
Even the devil finds it too cold
Rime-covered spikes of grass
Talk softly under our feet
Is this how fairy tales are born?
Poetry comes easily to those who
See the flakes of snow
Tremble from naked twigs.
In the mellow sunlight their fire sparkles.
Never have ancient riverbeds
Given up such diamonds.
Love cuts their facets into my enemy
Everlasting memories.

WASTED WOLF WHISTLES

Her clothes are chic, her skin is clear,
she knows no doubt and shows no fear
Men find her desirable
her figure's admirable
Many a suitor tried his luck
she laughs as each becomes unstuck.

Men learn to take it on the chin
when told she cannot fit them in.
Her schedule's full, her life's complete
she will not email, blog or tweet
there's not a moment when she's free
there's hardly time to eat or pee.

Like her, a trillion grannies from Peru,
across to Bruges and Timbuctu,
from Capetown to St Petersburg,
they don't possess one selfish urge.
These grandmas, pleased to do their bit,
are always there to babysit!

Economies would collapse
if there were no babies on their laps.

50

DADDY-LONG LEGS (Crane Fly)

Daddy-longlegs
tries to stay airborne
without success.
The draught
makes his wings useless.
He lands on the stone floor
Legs – a child's first scribble.
He trembles,
scrunches up and lies still
like a piece of discarded cotton.

THE SPEC BUILDER

Spending money hurts my pocket.
Don't put in that extra socket
save on windows, make them smaller
and that fence need not be taller.

Don't use bricks if wood costs less;
spending money gives me stress.
Yes, that land came rather cheap.
Flood defences? They will keep.

Floods occur not every year
and may never reappear.
All my houses sold again
Job well done, I'm off to Spain.

THE DEMISE OF THE HOUSE OF LORDS
(Often proposed. What if?)

I sob, I ululate, I cry;
I cannot keep this paper dry.
This is a wicked, horrid day;
We Noble Lords are thrown away!

We'll no more hear that soft, 'Wake up.'
(Must Peers sleep only in their club?)
No more that gentle tug at sleeve;
'The House is Voting, I believe.'

What misery, what cruel intent;
My soul is crushed, is this the end?
Oh, flood, my filling, spilling eyes,
Cry for our House of Lord's demise.

THE BURLY COP

A burly cop sat on a bench
And watched a cobbler with a busty wench
   With a high-hop! The burly cop!

The burly cop he began to get hot
As he watched the cobbler's hairy bott'
   With a high-hop! The burly cop!

The burly cop pulled out his gun
And called to the cobbler, 'Stop your fun!'
   With a high-hop! The burly cop!

At the cobbler he aimed, but not very good,
The bullet went through his own left foot.
   With a high-hop! The burly cop!

'Zooks!' quoth the cobbler, 'How do you do?
Methinks you'll need a new left shoe.'
   With a high-hop! The burly cop!

As the cop collapsed on the bench,
'Let's go,' the cobbler said to the wench.
   With a high-hop! The burly cop!

THE BLUE-ARSED BLOWFLY

While studying at Domini
With lots of boring books,
I caught a blue-arsed blowfly
And kept him for his looks.

He looked like Doctor Shelley,
Except not quite as glum.
He had a rainbow belly
And a lovely rainbow bum.

I kept him in a jam jar
And fed him bits of bread
I let him fly, my rainbow star
At the end of a pink silk thread.

One day my blue-arsed blowfly
Just upped and went and died
I then felt such a lonely guy
That I just upped and cried.

On reading about experiments to breed chickens without feathers, so that more energy would be directed to growing meat instead of feathers.

NAKED AND COLD

Dear Lord, I get cold.
You gave the sheep a woolly coat
and something like it to the goat,
the lion you gave skin and fur
and likewise to the humble cur.
But I, if I may tell you somewhat bold,
find in the morning I get cold.
If you in your all-powerful way
could add some detail please, I pray.
We could have skin as thick as leather
to give protection 'gainst the weather.
Or give us feathers, if you wish
or even scales then like a fish.
But please do something if you care
for we're too naked as we are.

Your maker speaks – and I know best.
I made you so I could in you invest
an over-active, king-sized brain
that with your body you'll sustain.
If you were feathered, woolled or furred
or on your body scales occurred
your brain would shrink to half its size
and you'd be only half as wise.
So be content you're not a goat
and knit yourself a big warm coat.

OBSESSION

I used to gather and collect,
Without much rhyme or intellect
A painting or a coveted antique
New acquisitions every week

Now suddenly I've lost that fire
Gone has the passion to acquire.
I was a slave to my possessions
Now, in a small way, try transgression,
It led to decadence my new obsession.

SING A SONG OF MILLIONS (War with Iraq)

Sing a song of millions spent on war each day
We may lose some soldiers, but someone has to pay
Iraqies in their gardens, counting out their worth
Zoom came a missile and wiped them off the earth.

When the war is over, we soon start to tell,
'Wasn't that a lovely war, didn't we do well?'
Bush sat in Camp David giving thanks to God.
Tony was his honoured guest; he gave war the nod.

Letter to the Editor

PUBLISHED!

For me July was very good
Because you published *Dangerous Woods*
And all the more to my surprise
My story won first prize.

So, trusting I would get the dosh
I happily replaced my Macintosh
I feel however I should mention
And bring this fact to your attention:

Each day I ran to get the post
Abandoning my egg on toast
In July my tale was on your pages
But week after week – no wages.

If this should reach you while you've sent my prize
Ignore these lines and I apologise.

All things do come to those who wait.
The cheque did come, just six months late.

TEATIME

Two dear lady-friends gently sipping tea.
Each thought: She's toffee-nosed — not quite like me.
One smiled excitedly, You've heard about Anne?

>Do tell what happened, was it a man?

I will not pass on tales, I never do.
I'll not tell a soul — but I must tell you.

>You know you can trust me — some more tea?

Anne was accosted by sailors, dead drunk.
She talked to a beggar, how low has she sunk?
Who knows what happened, I don't care to guess.
Believe what you will, my dear, such a mess.

>I'm truly shocked, I am — some more jam?

Well dear, the police came cruising along,
While somebody sang a jolly rude song.
Two were arrested, and put in the van.
It was rather dark — one could have been Anne.

>My God, what fun — uh — one more bun?

Poor dear Anne, one can't help wondering why.
But we both know, she's not like you and I.

>I agree, I'm very . . . time for a sherry!

ABC OF LIFE

A   for Adultery; that's marital pingpong
B   for Bible, a book that's far too long
C   for Catholics who do believe in God
D   is for Dawkins who certainly does not
E   for Erotic which readies you for play
F   for Flatulence when beans have their way
G   is for Government at best when it is least
H   is for Hangover; payment for the feast
I   is for Idiot who could be me or you
J   for Jacuzzi that's always best for two
K   for KitKat, the food that rots your teeth
L   is for Lady who's mostly underneath
M   is for Masculine, such fellows are quite rare
N   is for Nincompoop, you won't admit you are
O   for Obsolescence in everything you buy
P   for Pie — look, there's one in the sky!
Q   is for Queenie whose speeches are damn good
R   for Rock and Roll, OK when in the mood
S   is for Sadists who like to beat your bum
T   for Tapestry to do when you feel glum
U   for Underpants not worn in Paradise
V   for Virgin; would you like one for a wife?
W   is for Winter when your tootsies get cold
X   for Extra you grab when you feel bold
Y   is for Youth, we know, wasted on the young
Z   or Zipper — why is it always undone?

GETTING PAID

Butchers get paid, Bakers get paid
And so do flour-faced Millers.
Tinkers get paid, Tailors get paid
And so do red-eyed Distillers.

Cardinals get paid, Caterers get paid
And so do leather-clad Wenches.
Soldiers get paid, Secretaries get paid
And so do Judges on benches.

Policemen get paid, do Poets get paid?
No, well, maybe after they're dead
They may get laid, but seldom get paid
Their bank balance tends to be red.

Why not give up, go straight to the pub
Forget about being a genius
Get into a hot tub, Ay, there's the rub
It really is quite serious.

When pen comes near paper
This poetry caper
Is a dangerous addiction.
Because you see, it won't go away,
You've got CPWA
The Compulsive Poetry Writing Affliction.

As read in the *Daily Mail*,
that goldmine of medical mysteries explained

DYSFUNCTION

Forty percent of men over forty
have real trouble at being naughty.
They suffer from a certain dysfunction.
When a man comes to this junction
it means, he no longer can do
what, as a man, he is expected to.

His GP will be most sympathetic
and even if he might be geriatric;
the little blue pills will be a success
bordering on the brink of – excess.

Lucky man. But why is there such neglect
of the sixty percent of men who, with respect,
are very well able to perform –
what is thought to be the norm.

Men are said to think of being amorous every minute
even when there might not be an opportunity to begin it.

Could science not devise a brightly coloured pill,
for those sixty per cent of men – that will,
when there's that untimely compulsion,
put a temporary delay on this overactive function?

PC POETRY

I'm writing an abstract, a nothing verse
with only inane words, no praise nor a curse
It's not about death it's not about living
it's not about taking and not about giving
it's not about heaven it's not about hell
it's not about feeling off colour or well

it's not about women naked or clad
let them be skinny or fat
let them be short or let them be tall
I'm not writing about any at all
you may be witty or may be a bore
whether all at sea or simply ashore

I'll not write about anyone, I flatly refuse
I will not insult and will not amuse
why should I be writing about princes or kings
about money, love, hate or such things
I'll keep to myself and pocket my pen
if I have an idea I will just count to ten

If I write about nothing, I cannot go wrong
except this verse went on far too long.

THE 32 HISTORIC CHURCHES OF NORWICH

So many medieval churches are still standing
what in heaven's name was God demanding?
What history, such care for our salvation,
but faith is now replaced by conservation.

There was a time each church was well attended.
It seems today that time has ended.
And yet each empty church, a touch dilapidated,
has found new life, new uses are created.

In one such shell a Spanish group will meet
to entertain whoever strays in from the street.
Another houses activities that vary
from knitting classes to a massage for the weary.

Another still hosts fashionable creations
sellers of books, old records and carnations.
I watch an artist as he paints a girl,
and corpulent young ladies as they twirl.

The church's organ's either gone or deathly silent
and yet each church is still a peaceful island.
Where psalms were sung and sermons preached
there's still a measure of contentment to be reached.

I may not want to worship when I wander in
as there is no priest I need not think of sin.
And for a time the sense of peace and stillness is still real
until developers replace them all with concrete and with steel.

DANGER ZONE

They're coming towards me three abreast,
charging ahead with no quarter or rest,
their strength is ferocious, get out of our way
see-nothing-cold-eyes that nothing will sway.

Advancing straight at me, unswervingly grim,
all pose equal threats, and all are equally prim.
Eyes fixed on the distance steadfast and firm
they'll not stop or swerve for human or worm.

Taking the pavement they sweep all before them.
I'm scared and I'm helpless, I t-tremble before them.
They push on at speed while in deep conversation
sow fear and panic, and reap consternation.

I leap to the side, I'm suddenly agile.
Prompted by terror, I jump half a mile
To save myself, I leap into the gutter
to stop being spread on the pavement like butter.

Then 'woosh!' go the strollers, I cringe as they pass,
and tremble like jelly, flat out on my arse.

Villanelle

THE FLY

I feel a tickling on my pate,
and slap my head at once, but no,
as usual I am too late.

The beast has flown, escaped his fate
he is too quick, I am too slow
I feel a tickling on my pate.

Ah, there he is, I'll get you mate!
I'll get him from behind, like so!
As usual I am too late.

Now, cunning, I decide to wait,
so watch him high, and watch him low.
I feel a tickling on my pate.

I suddenly then, blind with hate,
like lightning, strike a mighty blow.
As usual I am too late.

I hear the blow reverberate
inside my skull. As down I go;
I feel a tickling on my pate,
as usual I am too late.

FOOTWEAR VILLAGE

I know a young lady who lives in a shoe
She's read Marie Stopes and knows what to do.

And Jill, down the hill, resides in a boot
Hiding from Jack, that randy old coot.

An elderly matron makes home in a pump
Fitting quite nicely, save part of her rump.

I quite like Tom Thumb, that cute little nipper
He likes to keep warm, so he's found in a slipper.

Bill has a hire-car with himself as the chauffeur
He's home-sitting now in a tan-coloured loafer.

Our lazy Dutch actor who sleeps like a log
On bedding of straw in a stout wooden clog.

A teenage page-three girl, running from scandal
Does like playing house in an open red sandal.

A recently arrived settler, pinkish of skin
Appears now quite happy in a soft moccasin.

A sun-burnt Aussie, a fair dinkum good cobber
Curls up in a red sweat-stained flip-flop-flopper.

Myself is known in these parts as virtuous old Jock
And as we've run out of footwear, I live in a sock.

KING ARTHUR

When good King Arthur ruled this land,
    He was a goodly king;
He killed three horses and a knight,
    To make a black pudding.

A black pudding the king did make,
    And stuffed it well with peat;
And in it put great lumps of coal,
    As big as my two feet.

The king and queen not ate thereof;
    But all the noblemen tried;
The poor chaps ate the lot that night,
    and all the next day died.

The king to the queen said, 'What a shame;
    I feel I am to blame.'
The queen said, 'Put them on the fire, my dear,
    They'll give a lovely flame.'

CALL YOURSELF AN EDITOR?

My boy's written many a verse.
I've read his best, and read his worst.
You know all Mums are cruel to be kind;
well, this one's perfect to my mind.

If you had looked at all his stuff,
You'd know it's more than good enough!
My boy's been robbed of praise and dosh,
Where many others read like tosh!

I've sent this verse as I am right,
It's better than your self could write.
Yes even Shakespeare at his best,
would rate this poem above the rest!

So publish it, you gadabout!
Or I'll come round to sort you out!

POLITICIANS

We talk to pretty nurses
And we respect the old,
Put a little in their purses
So they'll survive the cold.

Though granny's on a trolley
And her op is twelve months late
We're spending so much lolly,
That soon she'll have a date.

You've had your vaccination
Or maybe even two
All right there's some inflation
But that's not all we do.

The homes we'll build one day,
Each with a bathroom and a loo?
Well, plans are almost on the way.
That's how we work for you.

So, do you want your future secure?
Just vote for us and we'll make sure.

THE DIAMOND *(Apologies to John Betjeman)*

Tough luck caught up with Lola, the singer;
when her sheepdog swallowed her ring.
She fished down its throat with a finger
to try to retrieve the lost thing.

But just as she thought that she had it
the pup took a big gulp of air.
Lola feared that the ring had gone forever.
She never had felt such a scare.

'That ring is my proof of engagement
Ollie gave it to me only last night.
He might cancel our wedding announcement
and probably leave me, he might!'

That night poor Lola did not sleep a wink
her thoughts went around and around
next morning, though not in the pink,
she still went walkies with the hound.

He walked up the very first tree,
to do a number two, Lola could see;
he always stopped for that on the Heath
and Lola smiled as something glittered underneath.

A TRUE STORY in 2011

Belinda was his high class cleaner who waved her skirt at him.
Jones, in his sprightly eighties noted, her body firm and trim.
She cooked his delicious meals for him and vacuumed every room.
She always had a smile for him and sweetly banished gloom.

He paid her in excess of what already was agreed,
Because he felt she did fulfil his every human need.
He had no relatives, so he promised her his house.
Jones truly asked the wench to be his wedded spouse.

He trusted her implicitly while she did all his banking.
but she took extra cash while Jones dreamed of a spanking.
The bank did send a statement that revealed the callous theft
She took ten thousand out and thought, there's still a good bit left.

She, with the cash, then went and booked a luxury cruising holiday.
When Jones confronted her, and yelled 'Be on your way!'
She cried hot tears, that stopped and then instead
She swung a cricket bat and broke the old man's head.

Then in the dark of night she dug a hole in Jones' yard
She heaved him in and stamped the filled in earth down hard
But neighbours who had daily met him on the street for years
Began to wonder how he was, so some expressed their fears.

One thing to another led and soon the tongues went wagging.
Police when called saw that a section of the lawn was sagging.
A little digging showed poor Jones was buried in that hollow
The arrest and conviction of his cleaner soon did follow.

In court she said, Your Lordship, I am quite innocent.
It was an awful accident that did befall my dear old friend.
The judge asked, 'Why did you not own up three months ago?'
'My Lord, my son was being wed. I could not let him know.

It would have spoiled his wedding. That's all it was, I swear,
And all the more I bought a hat and dress to wear.'

GETTING OLDER

I've never been brilliant at remembering names,
thinking William is Charles – or was it James?
I recall Neville as Nigel and Alice as Anne
and McKane I am sure is really McCann.

My memory's going but what do I care,
my name is Johannes to this I can swear.
Hello Mrs Miller, how nice and how splendid.
I am Mrs Mason – that friendship has ended.

My memory's gone and I wish I knew where,
my name is Johannes, I think, no I swear.
I remember Pete West from when I was ten
but who was that chap I shook hands with just then?

I even remember my two best friends aged seven
one was called Ken and the other was Kevin.
But today when I see a familiar face
I say, Hello Jo, and she says, No, I'm Grace.

Ah, well, I am Johannes and that is the end
Yes, I am pretty certain, say – ninety per cent.

CHRISTOPHER TYE (±1497-1572/3)

That peevish man, Christopher Tye,
composer and of humour rather dry,
Master of Choristers, Doctor of Music,
played for royalty and the public.

In fifteen-sixty, more or less,
he played the organ for Queen Bess.
Bess, pulling faces like a prune,
'Tell Doctor Tye he's out of tune.'

So up the verger went to Tye,
who sniffed and snorted this reply:
'Tell Her Most Gracious Majesty, I fear,
't is not my playing out of tune, but 'tis the Royal Ear.'

AN OLD LADY

There was an old lady who lived in a sandal
without electricity, just a candle.
Seventeen kids to feed each day
she tried and tried but could find no way.

A man came by and she asked him in.
While the poor sod had thoughts of sin
she tickled him once then took all his money.
That night her kids had bread and honey.

Nothing happened remotely pudendal
he kept his mouth shut for fear of scandal.

MARY

Mary, Mary, quite contrary
how did your nose get so straight?
A little chip here and a little chop there
that's how my nose was made.

Mary, Mary, quite contrary
how did you get that smile?
With a little bridge here and a little cap there
that cost me quite a pile.

Mary, Mary quite contrary
where did that big bum go?
A little cut here and a little suck there
that's what made it so.

Mary, Mary, quite contrary
how did those boobies grow?
A little snip here and an implant there
that's what made them so.

Mary, Mary, quite contrary
how did you pay for that ring?
With a cuddle here and a snuggle there
that's how I paid for everything.

FINGER PLAY

Round about, round about
Here she sits bare.
In the corner of the cornfield
You will find her there.

This little digit teased her,
This little digit pleased her,
This little digit measured her,
This little digit pleasured her,
And to this little digit she said,
'Now you'll have to marry me.'

FEELING TOO WELL

I can't feel that pain in my back,
And the knee that I cracked
Performs like a well-oiled hinge
My dodgy hip? Not a twinge.
My tummy, my chest?
Every pain has gone West.
When I give it a twist
There's no strain in my wrist
I am worried! Am I still alive?

Then, a breath of relief;
Sneaking up like a thief,
There's a hint of a pain up my nose.
Which now spreads all the way to my toes.
I am happy! I must be alive.

POET'S LAMENT *for two voices*

I do write poetry, but I suffer from a cold at present.
               That's unpleasant
My throat is so sore
               what a bore
My back is aching
               you're faking
I'm coughing like mad
               you poor lad
My tummy's upset
               something you ate, let's call . . . the vet
My knees are creaking,
how do I write with my bladder leaking?
My teeth are falling out.
               at least you don't have gout
but I ache throughout!
I feel depressed, stressed!

Believe me, all my poetry turns to doggerel
or verse in this state
               I could get a doctor.
I fear it's too late.

DO I HAVE TO?

Will I have to be sexy at sixty?
Will I have to keep trying so hard?
Will I have to be naughty at sixty?
Let's think of the strain on the heart.

Will I have to be sexy at sixty?
And pretend that I am still thirty-five,
Will I be an old devil at sixty,
Or maybe just glad I'm alive.

Will I have to be sexy at sixty?
And prove that I am still very hot
I may sometimes be sexy at sixty,
But mostly decide that I'm not.

DREAM POETRY

Last night's dream was exciting
Suddenly I was writing
with a pencil in each hand
twice as fast, you'll understand
with my right of work and strife
with my left of love and life.

Left and right the words came fast
until the page was full at last.
Tired, I gave the muse my thanks.
When I woke the page was blank.

LITTLE BO-PEEP

Little Bo-peep never loses sleep
when her boyfriend leaves after a fight,
leave him alone and he'll come home.
She'll enjoy watching Telly that night.

Little Bo-peep fell fast asleep
and dreamt that she saw him cheating.
When she awoke she found it a joke
and there he sat quietly eating.

But still she took her little crook
determined to hit him it seems.
She did so indeed and made the poor chap bleed,
to make him behave in her dreams.

It happened one day, Bo-peep too did stray
in a meadow not very far.
There she was spied with a boy at her side,
by the boyfriend who watched from his car.

He heaved a sigh and wiped his eye
and over the hillocks went rambling.
He did what he could, what a shepherd would
and chopped off the head of his lambkin.

UNUSUAL PRONOUNCIATIONS

Anne lived in Bicester with her sicester
when Jill went away Anne badly micester
but when Jill came home again
Anne was happy then,
embraced her and happily kicester.

There was Libby living in Leicester
whose husband wanted to teicester
he said, 'Be more extrovert.'
But then called her a flirt
and then mercilessly moleicester

The Count said, 'Please call me plain Mr,'
to the innocent girl as he Kr.
'and I thought that you might
stay with me tonight.'
She said, 'I'll first phone mummy in Br.'

MRS

At the party me and Jones' Mrs
never thought that anyone would mrs,
But just as we had our fun
Jones came in with a gun
I ran for my life from the prem-mrs.

THE ABC OF WAR (1)

A is for Army that's like a family once you're in
         Armour plate that's often far too thin.
B is for Barracks where soldiers get tucked in
         Bullets that bite through your skin.
C is for Chests where medals can be stuck
         Carnage for when you run out of luck
D is for Dashing you will be in uniform
         Decapitate which can become the norm.
E is for Evening when you're dreaming in your bed
         Eternity! That's how long you will be dead.
F is for Family who are so far away
         Friendly Fire "So sorry," is what they'll say.
G is for Generals who like to plan the battle
         Government that feeds you tittle-tattle.
H is for Home which you hope to see once more
         Hell of blood and shit and gore.
I is for Inspiration, why you signed up on the spot
         Invincible which you now know you are not.
J is for Jokes in letters to your mummy
         Jab with a bayonet in your tummy.
K is for Keep fit it's the army's good clean fun
         Kalashnikov a cheap and nasty gun.
L is for Love life which you have to put on hold
         Landmines, for stepping on, I'm told.
M is for Mates who often save your life
         Memories plague you for the rest of your life.
N is for New Beginning promised when war is won
         Nuclear Weapons we can depend upon.
O is for Optics, with some, you see at night
         Overkill that proves we're in the right.
P is for Peace that will come one day
         Potshots that may put you away.
Q is for Queen and country wherefore you fight
         Questions, can any war be right?
R is for Rifle your very best friend
         Rotting flesh with smells that offend.

S is for   Soldiers on parades we may admire
           Shit-scared during enemy fire.
T is for   Taught-Techniques that broaden your mind
           Torture? There are many kinds.
U is for   USA so brave to go to war
           UN – who knows what that is for.
V is for   Variety, the army has the touch
           Vietnam – it never taught us much.
W is for   the War that's easily won
           the War that will go on and on and on.
X is for   eXit that's when we get out
           eXterminate that's final without doubt.
Y is the   Yen for home, you'll phone mum and dad
     that Yellow-streak you didn't know you had.
Z is for   Zing, for vitality and zest
           Z-i-n-g!! that bullet in your chest.

THE ABC OF LOVE

A	is for Adulation when love is blind
B	is for Bliss that can only be in the mind
C	is for Casanova a dead Italian rake
D	is for Desire, something you can't fake
E	is for Eve, that first temptress in paradise
F	is for Fool when your feelings are unwise
G	is for Garlic the ultimate no-no
H	is for Haystack is that the place to go-go?
I	is for Icicles when love gets cold
J	is for Jealousy when young marries old
K	is for Kissing that's always a good start
L	is for Loss – so what?, it's only your heart
M	is for Magic when you're under love's spell
N	is for No which may mean yes as well
O	is for Obsession a persistent idea
P	is for Pain when Love does flee
Q	is for Quick when it's moving too fast
R	is for the Reckoning when the die is cast
S	is for Super sure, when you buy the ring
T	is for Temper which is not a good thing
U	is for Under when you want to be on top
V	is for Victoria, "We are not amused, so stop!"
W	is for Wonder when love comes without warning
X	is for Xtra when first you stay till morning
Y	is for Yearning when you want to Yield
Z	is for Zimmer frame! . . . No more playing the field!

SHORTS SECTION

The following verses are all short and short-short.

Love is a many-gendered thing.

I wish my grandpa would get his face out of my mirror.

Remember: A turkey is just for Christmas.

You may think biltong is smarter
As a starter
I prefer the oyster,
It's moister

Verbal messages are not worth the paper they have not been written on.

HAIKU
Ski like hell good sport
Apres ski more good
Home without break bones best

The Clerihew is named after its inventor Edmund Clerihew Bentley. A pseudo-biographical quatrain, rhymed as two couplets, with lines of uneven length more or less in rhythm of prose. It often contains or implies a moral reflection of some kind. The name of the subject supplies the first line.

CLERIHEWS

Napoleon Bonaparte:
Said 'Taking Russia proves quite hard.
Perhaps I'm getting old;
I really cannot stand this bloody cold.'

Princess Margaret,
Sometimes forgot about etiquette.
She liked holidays, lobsters and sin
and last but not least liked a nice drop of gin.

Jonathan Aitken, ex-minister.
Was there something slightly sinister?
Was it all above board?
No matter now, he's got lucky and found the Lord.

Kurt Waldheim said,
'I was young at the time.
The Nazi uniform was smart,
and really, I'm a nice fellow at heart.'

More Clerihews

Bill Clinton
Liked ladies with tight-fitting kit on.
We know what he meant.
But Bill was the president.

Oedipus the king
did an awful thing
killed his Dad in a fit of road rage
then married his Mum; didn't ask her age.

- - -

Eenie, meenie, miney, mo
I can't help but love you so.
I'll go East and I'll go West
North and South without a rest.

You're my woman, I'm your boy;
I'm your serious wind-up toy.
I'll go where you want me to
as long as mummy's coming too.

- - -

Little Jack Horner
sat in a corner
eating an onion pie
with beans that were tinned,
and when he broke wind
he said, What a big boy am I.

A SELECTION OF LIMERICKS

A bishop knelt in his consistory
to ask God to solve a small mystery.
He said, 'I can't quite see
how You're One and You're Three,
so how do we manage predestiny?'

A dentist correcting a bite
made errors, fortunately all slight
he put in the nice filling
for a girl who was willing
to let him go filling all night

Riding a stallion can be risky
You might attempt it, full of whisky.
But you'd be foolish if you dare
To ride him past a broody mare,
Especially when both beasts are frisky!

A geneticist created a three-headed fellow
one black head, one white head, one yellow.
His heads would discuss,
while he rode on the bus,
Longfellow, Saul Bellow, Novello.

The surgeon who lifted my face
Said, 'Ev'rything's now in its place,
So does it feel right?'
I said, 'No, it's too tight.'
'Okay, we loosen it then in that case.'

A matron in an art gallery crowd
broke wind in C flat, rather loud.
She started singing a tune
from the film Brigadoon,
but most of the crowd still went out.

A farmer in pink corduroys
did make an embarrassing noise.
His Stetson fell off
as he pretended to cough.
It's one of his often used ploys.

A matronly lady said ouch!
when she sat on a pin on the couch
she said, 'Oh that sharp pin
penetrated my skin
but it's cured me from being a slouch.'

There was a young oldie, retired
whose friends had all long since expired
at a hundred and one
he still managed some fun
though he did get a little bit tired.

A lady who had second-sight
saw a vision of her husband one night
he had said he worked late
but she saw him and his mate
doing things that she thought were not right.

A devout virgin who had second-sight
was thrilled to see God late one night
But He said, 'It's my perception
that for immaculate conception
unfortunately you are much too tight.'

There was a young lady named Bunny
whose nose was continuously runny
nothing would work
till she thought of a cork
it made her look stuck-up and funny.

The Pope said to Cardinal Cometti
tonight let's not have plain spaghetti.
I spoke to the Lord
who said we can afford
one half dozen plump putti.

My auntie reached seventy-five
but never enjoyed being a wife
she thought my uncle
an ugly carbuncle
so lanced him one night with a knife.

A nasty young chap just for fun
decided to pick on a nun.
But he found out she held
a karate black belt
and she served the chap up in a bun.

JACK SPRAT

Jack Sprat could eat no fat
His wife could eat no lean
and so between them both, I saw
them lick the platter clean.

Now Mrs Sprat liked a bit of that
but Jack liked a bit of the other.
He pestered her and molested her
And now he's back with his mother.

- - -

We apologise for slavery
and other acts unsavoury
But wouldn't it be nice
if women would apologise
for eating that apple in paradise?

- - -

Rub-a-Dub,
Three girls in the club
And who would the fathers be?
The Butcher, The Baker,
The Candlestick Maker?
They've all run off to sea.

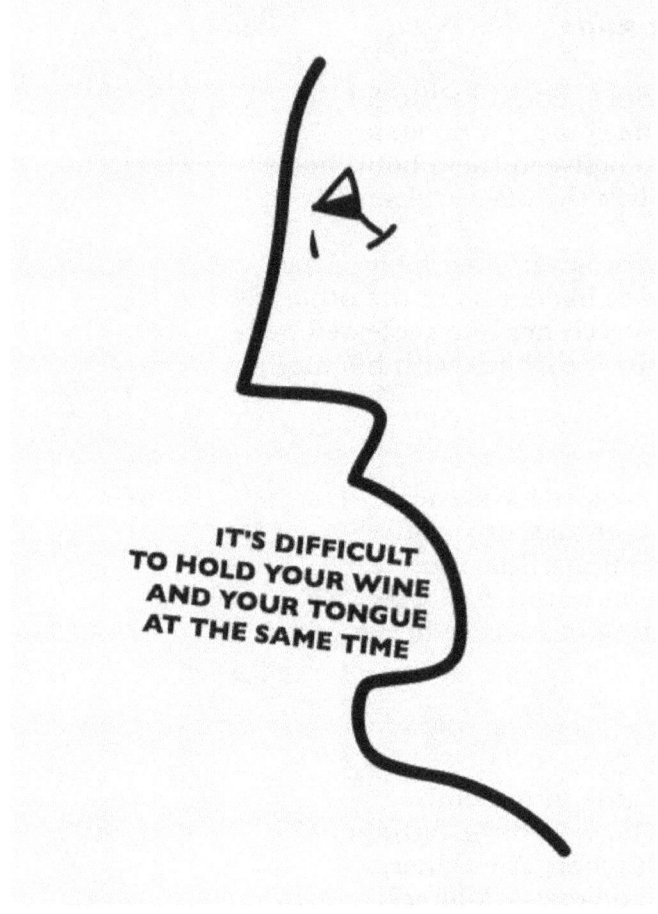

MORE LIMERICKS

A monk working on his salvation
bit off his left arm in frustration
He ranted, he raved,
"I'm saved, I'm saved!
And it's quicker than flagellation!"

A caretaker at London Zoo
as a sideline sold elephant's poo
for ladies' pretty window boxes
with geraniums, daisies, marigold and phloxes.
Politely he would ask, 'One lump or two?'

An old witch on firecracker night
Got onto her broom and took flight
Two rockets, two zoomers
Went right up her bloomers
Which instantly filled up with shite.

A poetry lover named Nelly
has two sonnets tatooed on her belly.
and on her back and her bum
you may read there, by gum,
The Ode to the West Wind by Shelley.

A rich sugar-daddy named Hirst,
whose nose-bubble threatened to burst,
said sweetheart come here
and I'll kiss you my dear.
Not so fast, she replied, safety first.

The village elder thought, thinking in Urdu:
'Why don't people do as I do?'
Then came to the conclusion
that life's an illusion
and all that while stuck in the loo.

A rich man married to Lydia
Said, 'Tell me how go I get rid'ya.
She said with a smile,
'The deeds to this pile,
and some cash or I'll contact the media'

A friendly young lady called Nelly
grew slightly concerned at her belly.
For each evening's new beau,
though she always said, 'No!'
her resolve that was firm turned to jelly.

A maiden from Golders Green Road
felt her fiancée resembled a toad
though she kissed him a lot
a prince he was not,
but financial potential he showed.

Miss Elsquith, quite timid and brittle
was seduced by a horrid lickspittle.
She said, 'I was mad,
I was used by the cad,
and to add to all that, he was little.'

THE CRAB

A mud crab, a giant crustacean
bit off a front leg in frustration.
He's the wonkiest crab in creation.

ORIGIN

Darwin maintained that our origin
did not begin with original sin.

And with much regret,
we must not forget,
though we feel we're sublime,
we started in slime.

- - -

Alone he walked in rain and cold
And strayed into the street where company is sold
He struck a bargain, so he thought
But she gave more than what he bought.

- - -

A masochist prone to irritation
bit off both his arms out of frustration.
He begged the sadist, 'Please bite off my head.'
The sadist smiled, 'First hug me,' he said.

THE EEL

The eel is quite a slippery fellow
His back is brown, his tum is yellow
He can be jellied, fried in batter,
But smoked he tastes a whole lot better.

ABC – Names of Persons Limericks

A hardworking cleaner named Alice
who lived and loved without malice
except maybe once
with a fellow named Lance
she became terribly jealous and callous

There's this very shy fellow named Bert
who when falling pretends he is hurt.
Ladies will to his joy
often fall for this ploy.
But wear jeans as he'll look up your skirt!

At midnight a fellow named Bate
was starving and thought, gosh it is late
so in his bed he just sitted
with his wool and he knitted
a chocolate croissant on a plate

There was a young fellow in Chester
Whose girlfriend begged him to molest her
He said I'm not sure,
'cause I think I'm too pure
But by then he'd already undressed her.

A frozen fellow named Clyde
had nostrils twelve inches wide
He sat on a log
and in jumped a dog
who found it quite slippery inside.

Dick Smith from Collaroy Heights
puts on grandma's stockings most nights
but I could see at a glance
that there was a good chance
he'd look much better in pink fishnet tights.

A very old friend called Evelyn
whose mouth is so big you can fit a telly in.
When she smiles you can watch
while she serves you a Scotch.
But she does not look all that feminine

There was an old man named Errol
who was happy and round as a barrel
he had many friends
but a size such as his tends
to give trouble finding apparel.

There was a young fellow named Franks
His tool tattoo was one of his pranks.
His mates all know it
And ask him to show it
Then think he's as thick as two planks.

There was a fat knight called Gawain
who despite twenty diets did gain
he decided at last
not to eat, only fast
it worked, but he slipped down the drain.

There was a young fellow named Hank
who never washed so he stank
He proposed to ten ladies
but never even got maybes
I wonder if that's why he drank.

Tattoed Horace, totally dead
never got to Heaven. Instead,
as the story will tell,
he was banished to Hell.
Should've read what Leviticus said.

A Swedish actor, named Iago.
Suffered with mumps and lumbago,
said his dear actress wife,
'For all of my sweet life
I'll not call you Iago, but Sven.'

A young man with great sex-appeal
Asked Jenny next door for a feel
She told him, 'Why not
You can have what I've got.'
But he said, 'I just wanted to check if it's real.'

There was a young fellow named Jack
who bartered his soul for some crack
the devil then chose
to double the dose
which blew Jack's head right off his neck.

Jeanette scorned the poet and said,
'You'll never get me in your bed.'
The poet said, 'Oh,
in that case I will go
and write some rude verses instead.'

A lovesick young fellow named Kevin
got permission to stay out 'til eleven.
But his girlfriend said, 'Tough,
I've no time to make love,
I have to be home prompt by seven.'

He told me he was, said young Luke,
a reincarnated bashi-bazouk*
this may sound quirky
but the words come from Turkey
and it sounds more like gobbleydegook.

*19th century Turkish soldier noted for brutality

There was a young lady called Lynn
who had a twin sister called Gwyn
it was rather hard
to tell them apart
except Gwyn drank vodka and Lynn drank gin.

Breakfast was served by Miss Lunt
where talk might quite often be blunt
when the bugle would sound
each went for his mount
and gathered outside for the hunt.

There was a young lady named Mike
who loved to do tricks on her bike
with her head on the saddle
and a hand on each pedal
she never looked quite ladylike.

A poetry lover named Nelly
has two sonnets tatooed on her belly
and on her back and her bum
you may read there, by gum,
The Ode to the West Wind by Shelley.

A generous gambler named Otto
won eight million pounds on the lotto.
He said, 'Here's ten,' to his mother
'and here's five,' to his brother.
'I'm off to drink myself blotto.'

There was a young actor named Quintin
who had a glass eye with a squint in
when he was asked to act
he disguised that small fact
and put on his specs with a tint in.

That jolly young oldie named Rex
felt clothes should be deemed unisex
one day trousers and shirt,
the next blouse and skirt.
But then he was brought up in Middlesex.

A trendy young lady called Rose
punched ten little holes in her nose
They said you're a fool
though it looks really cool
but you sprays everyone when you blows.

There was this young fellow named Saul
who kept walking into a pole
He said, 'I must stop that
'cause my nose is getting flat.'
Then he promptly fell into a hole.

Thought that old playboy named Ted,
'Pretty soon I will die and be dead.'
He gathered his kin
and said with a grin,
'I'm five hundred thou in the red.'

An angelic toddler Tobias
grew up extremely pious
He grew seven feet wings
made of feathers and strings
and honest – he often flies by us.

There was a tall lady called Ursula
whose nose was exceedingly angular
it was sharp as a knife
and the love of her life,
while kissing, was stabbed in the jugular.

There was a stout woman named Vicky
who looked very nice but was tricky
meeting fellows with money
she'd be sweeter than honey
and cling to them as if she was sticky.

There was a young lady Wilhelmina
who committed a small misdemeanour
she swam totally bare
in the pond on the square
apart from me nobody has seen her.

A modern lady, Xantippe*,
always gave her Socrates lippe.
But with tucks and with nips
that took care of her lips
he implanted a lockable zippe.

*The wife of Socrates – proverbial as quarrelsome

There was an old girl called Yvette
went out in the rain and got wet
she was quite a sight
with her hair sleek and white
when in the morning she'd been a brunette.

Old Yolanda who lives on a boat
discovered a hole in her coat
she said 'Ah that will be handy
when I am feeling randy
but I better not tell my old goat.

There is a stout fellow named Zack
who flies across to New York and back
he wears superglued wings
and brings back contraband things
but a customs man watched him unpack.

ABC – Names of Places Limericks

There was a young sheila in Alice
whose boyfriend had cause to be jealous
After he'd shot her he said,
'Such a shame that she's dead
As I never bore her no malice.'

An elderly girl from Axminster
didn't want to be known as a spinster
she was certainly not loose
so she did pick and choose.
a carpenter, a printer and a sprinter.

A desperate young chap in BA
made a lovely girl out of clay
when he kissed her she woke
and then said, here's the joke,
So sorry dear boy, but I'm gay.

An industrious smithy in Birkin,
makes codpieces to any size gherkin.
The design for the bard
is of course fire retard
and there's space to fit unfinished work in.

A guru chap in Calcutta
hates all cheeses, meat and butter.
In principle that's fine
but no cigars or red wine?
Does that make him a saint or a nutter?

An aunt of mine living in Chard
was totally obsessed by de Sade
inspired by his book
she tortured her cook
and made him into a juicy roulade.

There's a musical student from Chile
with ambitions that border on silly
Could he play? Not a note.
Could he sing? Like a goat.
But he'll offer a hug when it's chilly.

A thirsty poor fellow from Chile
has a Gordian Knot in his willy
he shows this curious wick
in the pub as a trick
he'll never go spare for a drink, will he?

A certain plump lady from Dorset
had trouble getting into of her corset
six workmen came by
heard her soft plaintive cry
and the six of them managed to force it.

A certain young lady in Ealing
proceeded to walk on the ceiling
her long skirt did, of course,
bow to gravity's force
which was, therefore somewhat, revealing.

A deserted maiden in Ellingstring
left by her fiancée, kept the ring.
Married and divorced a new spouse
this time kept the ring and the house.
She's very ready for another fling.

A sprightly old fellow in Eton
loved ladies with plenty of meat on
so he gave the eye
to a widow nearby
but she had a young chap she was sweet on.

A middle-aged man in Eau Claire
loved dancing with the cuddly au pair
Of course they went further
so his wife planned their murther
but before that they ran off to Bonaire.

A clever mechanic in Ebano
had married a voluptuous soprano.
When she said come to bed
he said, 'Don't be mad
but I'm still playing with my Meccano.'

A talented butcher in Follifoot
found life was treating him jolly good
a nice piece of meat
always worked quite a treat
and if Polly would not, Molly would.

A church-going maiden in Flitton
could not find an empty pew to sit on
she asked young McGee
could she sit on his knee?
'Yes as long as you're keeping your kit on.'

The handsomest lawyer in France
at a party drew many a glance.
His hostess said, 'My dear
I'm so glad you are here
do you fancy the maid, me or young Lance?'

Two elderly felons in Grateley
live in a home, very stately.
Retired from violent crime
they collect clocks that chime
and only do occasional frauds lately.

I grew up in a small place called Gin Gin
And spent most of my youth reading Tin-tin
Till a lady called Jo
Taught me all that I know
It's the town where I first learned to sin in.

An ancient bearded man in Goa
felt he was the re-incarnation of Noah.
So he built a canoe
out of matchsticks and glue
and set sail via Samoa and Genoa to Balboa.

A long suffering preacher in Ghent
to his wife said, 'It's not what is meant
by giving love to all men.
You've loved Ken, Ben and Len,
and all within two days of Lent.'

A six-year old boy in Hannover
said, 'I am the new Casanova
when I stop sucking my thumb
I will marry my mum
and daddy will have to move over.'

A well-read young man from The Hook,
each morning would speed-read a book
Each night he had a new hero,
he'd pretend to be Nero,
or St Paul, or perhaps Captain Cook.

There was a young farmer in Hove
who had twenty-five cows, which he drove
all the way into Brighton
for all to set eyes on,
but he always left one on the stove.

A middle class miller from Hove
thought he was no other than Jove
but let's not get ecstatic
for he was quite erratic
he scared us by the way he drove.

An enterprising witch from Ipswich
connected herself to a dip switch
her broomstick at speed
would buck like a steed
and she yelled, 'Keep her steady you bitch.'

A rickshaw owner in Indonesia
suffers from bouts of amnesia
when he speaks to his wife,
anyone out of five
are you Delia, Ophilia, Celia, Lelia or Alisia?

There was a young farmer from Icklesham
who had his way with the girls and tickled them.
He finally fell down
with jolly Miss Brown,
who cuts off men's bits and pickles them.

An idle young fool in Jarrow
fell madly in love with a sparrow
but the sparrow said, 'Twit
I prefer the great tit.'
So he shot the poor sparrow with an arrow.

A fussy young oldie from Kent
a well-dressed fastidious gent
ran plump out of luck
when his zipper got stuck
on an expensive mixed daytrip to Ghent.

A frugal chemist from Kos
had the idea of recycling floss
although it was clean
it always looked green
as it never failed to grow moss.

A glitzy young lady from Lille
driving her new automobile,
mowéd down a garçon
and chimed, 'Mon Dieu, pardon,
I 'ope you non damage my veel.'

A chicken farmer's wife in Mucking
never slept for the noise of the clucking.
Fed up, the farmer said, 'Right
I will kill them tonight
as long as you help with the plucking.'

A white-robed gent sailing the Nile
Said, 'Gosh this river smells vile.'
His mate said, 'You're right
it's probably shite
but still, we are travelling in style.'

A tourist near Notre Dame
was pestering a small French madame
he said, 'Are you of the night?'
she said 'No, but I fight,'
And broke both his legs and an arm.

A nubile young lady from Ndola
for effect always wore a pink bowler
she could sing, she could dance
and when she had the chance
would breakfast on beetroot and cola.

A single young man in Oman
sighed deeply and whispered, 'Oh man
I'm sure it's illegal
to be in love with an eagle
but I'm just doing the best that I can.'

A limerick about Omsk, it's a pity
no words will rhyme with that city
so don't ask for that letter
I'll do others better
I refuse to do Omsk, so, tough titty.

A jolly young wife in Occold
made her husband into a cuckold
so he killed her stone dead
'I did it,' he said
'as I had become somewhat disgruntled.'

An ambitious musician from Piddle
was born without having a middle
yet he never looked glum
with his chin on his bum
but he always looked right with his fiddle.

A elderly lover from Qatar
made love while driving his car
his young mistress screamed, 'Pop,
put the brakes on and stop
we're crashing into the Kasbah!'

A certain young lady in Rome
invited me into her home.
She looked a delight
but I found out that night
her curves were all fashioned of foam.

A cute lady from Rome, I believe
never wore her heart on her sleeve
she had plenty of class
and tattooed hearts on her arse
where 'twas pinched by a young lad called Steve.

That well-upholstered lady in Rome
who enhances her curves with foam
when she passes on her bike
she wobbles, which I like,
but I never follow her home.

A minister's wife from Roche
talked twiddle-twaddle and tosh
she said, 'Drat it and bum.'
all the while chewing gum
then forgot herself and said, Gosh!

A giant in the place called St Issey
was shy and exceedingly prissy
his mother said, 'Lad
you are born to be bad.'
He said, 'Oh please mummy give me a kissy.'

A bad tempered old cat from St Ives
was inordinately fond of fresh chives
his owner said, 'Lad
you sure do smell bad.'
I'm tempted to take some of your lives.

A rustic old man in Sabanilla
flavours his cigars with vanilla
we know what he thinks
but we think that they stinks
so we keep well away from his villa.

A nouveau riche man in Sassafras
whose name is not true but an alias
he calls himself Jake
yes we know that's a fake
but his parties are always first class.

An ardent young lover from Shove
Cut off both his ears out of love.
They said, 'Can you hear?'
He said, 'If you're near,
and my bowler now fits like a glove.'

There is a man from Totton
whose body is made of cotton.
Each day he will ingest
a shirt or a vest
he'll die when his cotton gets rotten.

A middle-aged fellow in Turkey
in excellent health and quite perky,
met a lady one night
and then gave her a fright
when she saw that his third leg was quirky.

A crazed fellow poet in Utterby
was obsessed by his wife so utterly
that all the poems he'd written
told of how much he was smitten
but she still thought him utterly nutterly.

A masochist shepherd in Vladivostock
walked around with a stone in his sock.
It got very sore
But he yelled, 'I want more'
and replaced the stone with a rock.

A confuséd preacher in Ventnor
had an owl who he saw as his mentor.
He asked, 'What shall I do?'
The owl said, 'Hoo-hoo.'
Good advice that the preacher went for.

A baker in old Venezuela
was madly in love with Consuela
he drank much from her cup
could not keep that up
like yesterday's bread, he'd gone stala.

There is an old lady in Wales
who smokes but never inhales
she loves cooking dinners
for weaklings and sinners
but only invites single males.

A solemn fellow in Whepstead
built an aeroplane out of a bedstead
and to his surprise
it moves and it flies
but never as high as the woodshed.

A lovesick fellow in Xanxeré
fashioned a girl from papier maché.
As her skin shines like lacquer
she was quite a cracker
but she broke while they romped in the hay.

That clumsy young thing from York
picked off her nose with a fork.
It made her look grim
but does help her to swim
as she has a big nose made of cork.

An ancient shepherd from Zeal
no longer musters up much sex appeal.
Yet a widow from York
thought him better than pork
And loved ringing his great glockenspiel.

A mechanical chauffeur in Zwiesel
is the size of a small painter's easel
he talks and reads maps
and is partial to schnapps
but slightly prefers warmed-up diesel.

A girl on the shores of Xingú
was told that navels unscrew.
In the Brazilian breed
they do so indeed
that's why their bums always look new.

AFTERWORD

If you keep *Frivolous Verses* by your bed,
It's sure to raise a chuckle when it's read.

Good Night
Johannes

ABOUT THE AUTHOR

Johannes Kerkhoven is an artist and author. Born in Rotterdam he spent the first nine years of his life in Franeker. During the war he lived in Hilversum and later in Utrecht before emigrating to Australia. He now enjoys living in Hove.

His MIXED CONCRETE – Visual Poetry was published in 2006.
His novel STATE OF GUILT 2019.
Short Stories STUFFED! 2021.

www.ingramcontent.com/pod-product-compliance
Lightning Source LLC
Chambersburg PA
CBHW022001100426
42738CB00042B/1172